Why the Bastille Matters
On The Road Toward Liberation

The French Revolutions of 1789, 1791, and 1793 changed the way the entire world thought about politics, the nation state, and the kind of rights those people who populate those nations are entitled to. Throughout the French Revolution, the nation gave way to one progressive faction after another until the conservative coup orchestrated by Napoleon Bonaparte. Which then ushered in the era of the First French Empire, and also the Napoleonic Wars. Although today I will put on exhibition one event out of that very perilous, yet glorious age that saw the first inklings of humanity's emancipation, or at least the idea of our emancipation. The event I shall be talking about is The Fall of The Bastille; for it was not only one of the most consequential moments that occurred during the French Revolution, but also one of the most consequential moments in human history. This was one of the few moments in human history that the majority of the unseen and unknown oppressed masses led themselves onto freedom, onto glory, and most importantly onto self-governance. It is one of the greatest tragedies that the incarnation of freedom is not constantly discussed at length. I believe that it is my duty to tell this most sacred story, and how it can give us hope for a better future. However, every grand piece of history equally deserves a grand prelude.

The Bastille was a Medieval French fortress which was located on the eastern part of Paris. It was later turned into a political prison by the Ancien Regime more widely known as the Bourbon Dynasty which lasted from 1589-1792, and then a second period of rule that lasted from 1814-1830. They were eventually permanently deposed by the Second French Revolution, or better known as the July Revolution. The problems that led to the First French Revolution are numerous. So, I will list ones that specifically relate to those that would most likely cause one to be a disgruntled citizen of France. More thoroughly put, somethings that would encourage one to act in a seditious manner against one's government. These things would be the massive lack of food for the common people. The imprisonment for those who spoke out, the complete economic stagnation, and runaway debt caused by foreign military expeditions.

Such as assisting the American Colonies in their Revolution.

Imagine having a government that is willing to send thousands of your fellow countrymen to go die for liberty in a foreign country that is located thousands of miles away yet denies you all of those liberties that they are fighting for. I hate to state the obvious, but this sounds a lot like the modern United States, let me explain. For the past twenty years we have constantly been waging ineffective, and extremely expensive wars across the Middle East fighting for "freedom and liberty".

All the while millions of Americans are living in abject poverty, as if they were living in a third world country. Most Americans are deprived of wages that would secure for them their basic needs.

Most Americans have trouble finding adequate housing for themselves and their families. Most Americans spend most of their days in a workplace that deprives them of their individuality and self respect. Most Americans are unable to secure funds and educate themselves in order to acquire a better life. Most Americans are unable speak their minds out of fear from corporate censorship. Most Americans who chose to speak out against the oppression that they live under, are then prosecuted under false pretenses and forced into either jail or public humiliation. So as American boys were fighting in Iraq, and in Afghanistan their fellow countrymen lived in oppression. Also similar to the Ancien Regime; the average American citizen is forced to choose between going hungry or eating poison disguised as food.

One explanation for such complete failure is the same as it was in Ancien France, for which I'll explain in two parts. The first part is the total lack of power that is currently possessed by the legislature. The legislature being the Senate, and the House of Representatives which is supposed to be the peoples main voice in government. However, currently this institution has little to no affect on the lives of their constituents, mostly due to the Bureaucracy that has been bought and paid for by the Corporate Aristocracy? The second problem is that the President and the Executive Branch along with the Bureaucracy at large acts in the manner of a despot or a tyrant to target those who dissent from the authoritarian ideology that now rules this once great Republic. Anytime the Legislature tries to help prevent its people from living in tyranny, and destitution; the Executive Branch and its Bureaucratic tentacles envelop the public conscious to ensure the continuous security of the Aristocracy and its wealth and power. They are unable to correct these egregious sins because of the Aristocracies financing of the electoral campaigns, there is a small minority of individuals who are buying our Representatives, and Bureaucrats to serve the needs of the affluent. These businessmen have turned our government into lackeys of the Cosmopolitan Bourgeoisie purposely disabling its original purpose of representing and protecting the people of the United States of America. This is eerily similar to what the Third Estate was subjected to, the King and the Clergy consistently imposed taxes on the Third Estate (which was composed of the middle and lower classes of the

French Kingdom), and then refused them the ability to petition the government, and then when the people protested, they were locked up.

This is why the Bastille was a prime target for the revolutionaries. On July 14, 1789, a group of French Patriot's had decided to go and break into the Hotel des Invalides and confiscate over 3,000 rifles and five cannons. They then marched off to the Bastille in order to acquire munitions. Why were the Frenchmen acting in such a troubling manner? Because in an attempt to destroy the rights of his people the King had just locked the doors to the Estates General which had been called to address the dire financial circumstances that the nation of France was facing at the time. The King and the French Aristocracy felt that they were under threat, so instead of allowing the people to reclaim their natural given rights as human beings they decided to fire his financial minister who tried to rein in spending. So then to add insult to injury he decided to place mercenaries all across the city in order to "maintain order". The Patriotic Frenchmen consistently requested that they be allowed into the fortress to free the prisoners, and also take the munitions which were stored inside of the fortress so that they could liberate the city of Paris from King Louis's Henchmen and also to show their disdain at the decision to cancel the audit of the government. However, the commander repeatedly dismissed the will of the people and refused to open the gates of the fortress.

Eventually the people broke through the gate only to be greeted by their oppressors with cannon fire. Then all of the sudden the tide had changed, and the Parisians quickly seized the cannons and turned them on the Bastille; the horrendous symbol of tyranny itself. They then broke through, freed the political prisoners, and finally secured the munitions they had fought so hard for. They then killed the Bastille's commander and paraded his head on a pike around the city. This was done in order to inform the people of Paris that they were now free from the despotism of the King, and the Wealthy Aristocracy, and they would now think twice before flaunting their privileges.

After this triumphant victory, they burned the Bastille down to the ground to ensure that the King would never strip them of their rights and lock them in that horrendous dungeon again. When King

Louis's advisors told him, the Bastille had just fallen he proceeded to ask the Duke de La Rochefoucauld; "So, is there a Rebellion?" To which he responded, "No, sire a Revolution!"

Here's why this is important; because there comes a time when a man can no longer accept oppression and despotism. He must take action into his own hands. The things I have discussed in relation to my own time and country are well known and understood as being objectively true in concern to the operations of our government and how it has been perverted.

However, it is hardly said out-loud in public. The reason for this is obvious, because just like the people of France who were once in fear of their government and were afraid to even criticize the powers that be; there were a few brave men who got the avalanche of liberty rolling. The first step is to say it out loud and accept the reality of our state and make a plan on how to change the system that oppresses us. The next step is to get others to realize they're being gaslighted by powers that do not care for their welfare. After this you have given society at large a choice, and this choice is to either accept your slavery at the hands of Cosmopolitan Bourgeois Industrialists, or to reclaim your rights that you were granted through the powers of nature and reason. Think of a Revolution like how you would think of a dry cleaner. Then think of our country like a tailored piece of clothing, and then think of our government as a bucket of mud that has been tossed onto the tailored piece of clothing. So, then the answer becomes clear that we must take the dirtied tailored piece of clothing to the dry cleaners.

This is why the people of France celebrate every July 14th 'Bastille Day' as the moment that the people of France broke the chains of being subjects of a monarchy and became citizens of a nation. What this demonstrates is that when a nation is enslaved by the powers that be, its only chance at freedom is to take matters into its own hands. Thus, it must tear down the towers of oppression that are in front of its progression as a Nation and as a Sovereign People. For the French it was the Bastille, for America it is the Cosmopolitan Bourgeois Global Capitalists. Take heart citizens and keep the dream of a Republic alive!

Vive Du Peuple

Vive Du Peuple

Viva La Revolution

Vive Le Nation

Vive La Republique

Gloire A Dieu

Liberte, Egalite, Fraternite

Fin